The Blindness of Biblical Betrayal

The Blindness of Biblical Betrayal

Bishop Joey Johnson

XULON PRESS

Xulon Press
2301 Lucien Way #415
Maitland, FL 32751
407.339.4217
www.xulonpress.com

© 2019 by Bishop Joey Johnson

All rights reserved solely by the author. The author guarantees all contents are original and do not infringe upon the legal rights of any other person or work. No part of this book may be reproduced in any form without the permission of the author. The views expressed in this book are not necessarily those of the publisher.

Unless otherwise indicated, Scripture quotations taken from the New American Standard Bible (NASB). Copyright © 1960, 1962, 1963, 1968, 1971, 1972, 1973, 1975, 1977, 1995 by The Lockman Foundation. Used by permission. All rights reserved.

Scripture quotations taken from the Holy Bible, New Living Translation (NLT). Copyright ©1996, 2004, 2007 by Tyndale House Foundation. Used by permission of Tyndale House Publishers, Inc.

Printed in the United States of America.

ISBN-13: 978-1-54566-748-4

The Blindness of Biblical Betrayal

Nothing is as painful and common as betrayal in the pastorate and church leadership! Yet, this topic is seldom discussed or preached about. I believe that is because of the dysfunctionality of the modern church. We seem to be more interested in entertaining and hyping people about a new season or an enlarged territory than helping them deal with real problems. Nevertheless, I have experienced betrayal several times and helped many others navigate the turbulent waters of betrayal.

In addition, betrayal blinds both the betrayer and the betrayed. This syndrome can only be seen through spiritual discernment.

What is even more disturbing is the fact that the betrayal usually comes from those that we have helped, invested in, and trusted the most!

And what's more, we are usually caught off guard.

Generally, we are completely surprised.

This raises several questions,

- "Why do those closest to us betray us?
- Why does betrayal seem to happen periodically?
- Why does betrayal continue to catch us so completely off guard?
- How do I handle betrayal?"

Of course, betrayal is not unique to the pastorate, but happens in the context of all relationships. The omnipresence of betrayal is captured in a several sayings that come to mind.

- Pastor Eddie L. Hawkins once said to me, "If you love people too much, they'll never forgive you for it!"
- Another saying is, "No good deed goes unpunished!"
- Malcolm X said, "To me, the thing that is worse than death is betrayal. You see, I

could conceive death, but I could not conceive betrayal."

- In one of his songs, the great hymnwriter of Israel, David wrote in

Psalm 55:12-14 (NLT2), "[12] It is not an enemy who taunts me—I could bear that. It is not my foes who so arrogantly insult me—I could have hidden from them. [13] Instead, it is you—my equal, my companion and close friend. [14] What good fellowship we once enjoyed as we walked together to the house of God."

David was betrayed by an intimate friend who regularly accompanied him on his trips to worship.

So, although I have periodically thought about betrayal across my 45-year career (2019), I recently began to give it more thought. I'd like to touch on one reason for betrayal, before exploring another.

First, perhaps we help some people more than we should, because we feel we are better than they are, and/or we enjoy being needed. This is certainly one possibility and a lot of this goes on. In his excellent and penetrating book, *A Model of Love: A Study in Philosophical Theology*, Vincent Brümmer paraphrases John MacMurray's teaching in *Persons in Relation*,

> "If in my relationship with you I insist on behaving generously toward you and refuse to accept your generosity in return, I make myself the giver and you the recipient. This is unjust to you. I put you in my debt and refuse to let you repay the debt. In that case I make the relation an unequal one. You are to have continual cause to be grateful to me, but I am not to be grateful to you. This is the worst kind of tyranny and it is shockingly unfair to you. It destroys the mutuality of the personal by destroying the equality which is its negative aspect. To maintain equality of persons in relationship is justice; and without it generosity becomes purely sentimental and wholly egocentric. My

care for you is only moral if it includes the intention to preserve your freedom as an agent, which is your independence of me. Even if you wish to be dependent on me, it is my business, for your sake, to prevent it."[1]

Leaders, whether we're talking about bishops, pastors, Sunday School teachers, or others, are often helpers who have not done their own work to get emotionally healthy. They know how to give, but they don't know how to receive and establish mutually respectful relationships.

This dysfunctional kind of relationship can lead to the one being helped rebelling against and betraying the one who is helping.

This is something that we should explore, but that would require deep psychological and spiritual discernment and would take us far beyond what I want to talk about in this book.

---

[1] Brümmer, Vincent, *The Model of Love: A Study in Philosophical Theology* (Page 161). Cambridge University Press. Kindle Edition.

There is another reason that is much more biblical, although it has <u>not</u> been recognized. It is what René Girard, French genius, anthropologist, philosopher, and theologian, entitled "mimetic rivalry." "René Girard was the world's premier thinker about the role of violence in cultural origins, and about the Bible's illumination of these origins and our present human condition."[2] He wrote nearly 30 books that cover many academic domains. In addition, there is a large and growing body of secondary literature on his work and influence that touch on such disciplines as literary criticism, critical theory, anthropology, theology, psychology, mythology, sociology, economics, cultural studies, and philosophy.

In fact, some doctoral students are doing their doctoral work specifically on Girard. My understanding of Girard comes from the ten books and several articles that I have read by him and on him. Girard was a genius and some of his teaching is esoteric, so I'll do my best to help you understand it.

---

[2] Girard, Rene, *I See Satan Fall Like Lightning.* (Page 11) Orbis Books. Kindle Edition.

The Blindness Of Biblical Betrayal

The word "mimetic," in Girard's thesis of "mimetic rivalry," come from a Greek word which means to imitate. Girard refused to use the word "imitate," because it did not capture the complex syndrome he was describing. He used the word "mimetic" in a much more systematic way to represent the negative imitation of acquisitive desire that goes on between people.

> Girard writes, "The principal source of violence between human beings is mimetic rivalry, the rivalry resulting from imitation of a model who becomes a rival or of a rival who becomes a model.... Mimetic rivalries can become so intense that the rivals denigrate each other, steal the other's possessions, seduce the other's spouse, and, finally, they even go as far as murder."[3]

People imitate each other and that imitation can lead to them being rivals!

---

[3] Girard, Rene, *I See Satan Fall Like Lightning.* (Page 11) Orbis Books. Kindle Edition.

(How does this happen?)

As people, we learn and are enculturated through imitating or copying, i.e. copying our family models and other models. In growing up, we not only imitate and copy behaviors, values, and other things, but we ingest and imitate the desires of our models. Yet, we are unaware of this mimesis. We consciously think our desires originate in ourselves.

I believe that God created us to learn through imitation. This may be seen in the fact that we are created in His image and His Son is the summing up and model of what humanity was intended to be.

In 1996, in Parma, Italy, Giacomo Rizzolatti's team of specialists in neuroscience made a chance discovery that made a huge contribution to Girard's mimetic research, i.e. by resonating with it. It was the discovery of mirror neurons. Mirror neurons are involved in the autonomic reaction of babies imitating the faces that their parents make at them. They found that a baby only two hours old will mimic anyone making a face over the bassinet.

A mentee, colleague, and friend of Girard, Jean-Michel Oughourlian, professor of clinical psychopathology at the University of Paris and chief of psychiatry at the American Hospital in Paris, writes about mirror neurons. Oughourlian makes the following observations:

- "Imitation is the first link, the point of departure for interhuman relations.
- It is the brain's mimetic property, represented by mirror neurons, that is at the origin of empathy, thanks to the 'mirrored' recognition of the other as 'like me,' my alter ego. It is empathy that makes it possible to decode and share emotions and feelings.
- It is by means of an innate mimetic mechanism that the human brain learns, understands, and integrates everything offered by the other, others, and the culture he is immersed in....
- We must emphasize the fact that the observer's mirror system reflects the

intention of the action he is witnessing, even if it is not completed."[4]

Based upon the anthropology of Girard, the research with mirror neurons, and additional research, Girard and Oughourlian created a new psychology. "Psychology" is science of the mind or mental life. This new psychology is put forth more completely by Jean-Michel Oughourlian. It is called "interdividual psychology." For the sake of ease, we'll call this "relational theology." Most American psychology deals with individuals as if people stand alone and their problems are in not being able to healthily stand alone, or to understand their individuality, or in allowing their individuality to be impinged upon, etc.

It may be interesting for you to know that I have been developing a relational theology, anthropology, and psychology for many years. In 1999, I did a sermon series entitled "The Doctrine of Relationships." It is the elaboration

---

[4] Jean-Michel, Oughourlian, *The Mimetic Brain*, Michigan State University Press, 2016, pp. 28-29.

of the implications of the New Testament concept of *koinonia*.

By the way, the Bible was written in a collectivistic culture and logic and nearly all historical cultures have been collectivistic. America is a rare exception to that history.

The individual maturity continuum proceeds from dependence, to independence, to interdependence. I propose that a collectivistic maturity continuum proceeds from dependence, to interdependence, to a healthy and relative independence. No person can be completely independent of all others.

Because of Girard and experience, I am arriving at a point of convergence in my theology, anthropology, and psychology.

This new psychology teaches that <u>no</u> one is a monad or a singular metaphysical entity from which material properties are said to devolve, in short, an individual.

Girard posits, from an anthropological basis, that we learn and grow from the models that we unconsciously imitate.

I'm reminded of the meditation of the English poet John Donne, which was written in the late 1500's.

> No man is an island,
> Entire of itself.
> Each is a piece of the continent,
> A part of the main.
> If a clod be washed away by the sea,
> Europe is the less.
> As well as if a promontory were.
> As well as if a manor of thine own
> Or of thine friend's were.
> Each man's death diminishes me,
> For I am involved in mankind.
> Therefore, send not to know
> For whom the bell tolls,
> It tolls for thee.

I rarely use the word "individual," because I believe it transmits to modern people that they are isolated units who need no one else. I use the term "persons," which indicates that we are always in relationship with others. In the Nicaean Creed, the members of the Godhead are called "persons," which is derived from the Latin word *persona*, which means the mask or appearance that one presents to the world. The three *personas* of Father, Son, and Holy Spirit are perichoretic, i.e. they fully interpenetrate one another and draw their identity from their Triune relationship. The Latin term used by the early Church Fathers was "circumincession." "Coinherence" is another synonym.

So, the problems that we are experiencing in America do not proceed from the fact that we are individuals who are different from each other, but that we are persons in collectives that are very much like each other and locked into dynamic relational interaction with others.

Relational psychology posits that each person's self-concept flows from the relationship. In America, we believe that our self-concept flows from some internal ontology or sense of being.

Oughourlian posits that we are in incredibly dynamic relational rapport with others. In that dynamic rapport, suggestion and imitation take place between the two persons or parties at an incredible frequency. The two persons or parties imitate each other unconsciously.

Consequently, our desires determine ourselves and our desires are "mimetic," i.e. they are imitated from others in a dynamic, ongoing, interaction with those in our lives. So, our desires really come from others, even though we perceive them as solely our own.

In our conscious worlds, we are aware of self and our desires and less aware or unaware that our desires flow from the desires of the models in our past and present.

In physical time, even though we are almost completely unaware of the source, the desires of our models lead to our desires, which lead to the makeup of self.

We are often in conversations where we walk away feeling the same as the other party without knowing that this has taken place.

This mimetic mechanism can lead to mimetic contagion where groups of people act in concert without knowing why they have done so.

Because we have had many relationships with many models, our self is comprised of many desires that we have imitated.

In short, we learn our desires from the imitation of others' desire. For example: I desire to learn, because both of my parents had a desire to learn. For most part, I was unaware of this, until I started reading Girard.

This imitation can entail learning and progress or, to the contrary, rivalry, conflict, or violence.

Okay! Here is a large point of application. Broadly speaking, the relation to the other can be broken down into three possibilities: the other as **model**; the other as **rival**; the other as **obstacle**.

Let's begin with the other as model. "When desire takes the other as a model without rivalry, we find ourselves in the framework of learning and friendship, that is to say in a situation of mutual, continuous, peaceful imitation-suggestion."[5] The relationship is guided by love!

---

[5] Jean-Michel, Oughourlian, *The Mimetic Brain*, Michigan State University Press, 2016, p. 58.

The Blindness of Biblical Betrayal

If the model is a sufficient distance from the model or mentor, either in physical distance or in social class, there is little tendency to rivalry. For example, we are generally too far away from God to consider Him a rival.

Okay! What about the other as rival? When the model and the disciple are close in proximity, desire, goals, etc. the model and the disciple may end up desiring and pursuing the same things and rivalry develops. It develops from envy and jealousy. The Old Testament teaches that we should not covet. In poverty stricken societies, this is not coveting of something like I have, but the coveting of the very thing that I have.

Our disciples often end up desiring the same spiritual things that we desire and blindly become our rivals.

Okay! What about the other as an obstacle? Girard discusses this by the term "metaphysical desire." "In Girard's view, mimetic desire (*i.e. the acquisitive human desire for what our models have*) may grow to such a degree, that a person may eventually desire to **be** his or her mentor. This is seen in the field of publicity.

Sometimes, consumers do not just desire a product for its inherent qualities, but rather, desire to *be* the celebrity that promotes such a product (*i.e. to be like Mike*). So, in metaphysical desire the disciple wants to be like the mentor and may come to want to be the mentor" (http://www.iep.utm.edu/girard/#SH2c).

While the closeness of a model and a disciple can lead to rivalry, "metaphysical desire leads a person not just to rivalry with her mentor, but total obsession with and resentment of the mentor. Consequently, the mentor becomes the main obstacle in the satisfaction of the person's metaphysical desire. Inasmuch as the person desires to *be* his mentor, such desire will never be satisfied. For nobody can be someone else" (http://www.iep.utm.edu/girard/#SH2c).

I cannot tell you how many times I have seen a disciple become so preoccupied with his/her discipler that s/he resents and eventually seeks to destroy the influence of that discipler.

So, the disciple renounces the model and wants to destroy the model.

The Blindness of Biblical Betrayal

Girard points out that saying one "No" to a disciple can precipitate this violence!

Later we shall see that this violence is in our DNA and this is narrated in the prehistory of the Bible in chapters 1-11 of Genesis.

Girard uses the biblical story of Cain and Abel to illustrate mimetic desire. Cain wanted what Abel had, i.e. his offering accepted by God. He eventually killed Abel to grasp what Abel had.

Even though Girard starts his biblical explanation with Cain and Abel, let's go back to where it all started, i.e. with Satan.

Satan desired the throne and the sovereignty of God. God had to say "No," because it was impossible for God to give Satan Himself. So, Satan became obsessed with destroying God. He trafficked among the angels and did damage to God's name attempting to usurp what God had.

It is important to note that although Satan seems to feel that God was intentionally withholding something from him, the only thing that God was withholding from Satan was Himself, which was not intentional but ontologically necessary.

Likewise, it was the serpent, Satan, who suggested to Eve that God was holding enlightenment and deity from them, "...for in the day that you eat thereof you shall be like God knowing good and evil."

We have no initial indication in the text that God was trying to make Adam and Eve God. He was making them Humans, in the image of God.

This kind of thinking may challenge you because of your paradigm and what you have been taught. Please allow me to give you a different view of Adam and Eve.

We attempt to read the Bible rationally and intellectually, and we do this in keeping with modern American culture.

Unfortunately, Genesis was not written as American history or science, but as theological "myth," not a story that is untrue, but a big story that explains why reality is the way that it is and how God should be viewed.

Some of the Church Fathers interpreted Genesis as spiritual allegory. An allegory is an extended metaphor. It is a story or symbol that uses characters or events to describe something else that it resembles.

Oughourlian interprets Genesis as psychological allegory. The story in Genesis symbolizes how humanity thinks.

God created the world for Adam and Eve, but in Adam's undifferentiated state, there was not another being corresponding to him. There was God and there were animals, but there was not another human being.

> Genesis 2:18 (NASB), "[18] Then the LORD God said, 'It is not good for the man to be alone; I will make him a helper suitable for him.'"

God differentiated Eve from Adam, brought her to Adam, and they were married! They were fully supplied by God and fully satisfied with each other; it was as if no one else existed in the world. They were in love! There was no one and nothing to separate them.

God was their model and they interacted with Him every day on their walks!

The Blindness Of Biblical Betrayal

So, what happened?

Genesis 3:1-7 (NASB), "[1] Now the serpent was more crafty than any beast of the field which the Lord God had made. And he said to the woman, 'Indeed, has God said, "You shall not eat from any tree of the garden"?' [2] The woman said to the serpent, 'From the fruit of the trees of the garden we may eat; [3] but from the fruit of the tree which is in the middle of the garden, God has said, "You shall not eat from it or touch it, or you will die."' [4] The serpent said to the woman, 'You surely will not die! [5] For God knows that in the day you eat from it your eyes will be opened, and you will be like God, knowing good and evil.' [6] When the woman saw that the tree was good for food, and that it was a delight to the eyes, and that the tree was desirable to make *one* wise, she took from its fruit and ate; and she gave also to her husband with her, and he ate. [7] Then

> the eyes of both of them were opened,
> and they knew that they were naked;
> and they sewed fig leaves together
> and made themselves loin coverings."

In this interaction between the serpent and Eve, we see the transference of mimetic desire. Before that point, Eve had no desires. All of her physical and relational needs were met. There was <u>no</u> psychological movement yet!

The serpent suggests that God was keeping something back from her that she should desire. He suggested that God didn't want Eve and Adam's eyes to come open and be like God. He suggests that being like God revolved around knowing good and evil, which meant eating from the tree that God had warned them not to eat from. It was the serpent, not God, who said, "God knows that in the day that you eat from the tree of the knowledge of good and evil you will be like God knowing good and evil."

You should know that ancient Church Father, Irenaeus, believed that Adam and Eve were created as children who were to grow into the image of God's only-begotten Son.

In truth, God was holding back from them the fruit of the knowledge of good and evil until they were mature enough to handle it. God was not saying, "No, not ever" but "No, not yet!"

Furthermore, God's instructions can be read more as a warning than a prohibition, "If you eat from the tree of knowledge of good and evil you will die. So, I advise you not to eat from it."

Eve imitated the suggestion of the serpent. In that moment, the devil became her model instead of God. In that moment, God became a rival and an obstacle to Eve fulfilling her desire.

Remember: all of this is an illusion in the mind of the one who is the follower or disciple. S/he sees the model as holding back something from him/her, even if that something is himself/herself.

It doesn't seem that the deed is fully done until Adam participates, because humanity is male and female. Eve offers Adam the fruit and he imitates her suggestion instead of God's suggestion. She becomes His model rather than God.

Consequently, when Adam eats the fruit, the eyes of both were opened. My father used to say, "It's a bad thing when a man's eyes come open!"

In mimetic rivalry, we come to want what we see our models want. We want to be the bishop, pastor, choir director, Sunday School, teacher, etc. When we can't get what we desire, or we can't get it when we want it, we resort to violence and even psychological murder to get what we want.

This paradigm, which explains the DNA of humanity, is seen throughout the Bible in

- Jacob and Esau;
- Joseph and his brothers, who were envious of the attention that Jacob lavished upon him.
- Both Aaron and Miriam were rivalrous concerning Moses' authority.
- Absalom and Adonijah coveted the throne of their father, King David.
- We see ongoing rivalry between the kings of Judah and Israel.

- The Chief Priest, Elders, scribes, etc., were envious of the religious authority and power of Jesus.
- Judas, who betrays Jesus (*we miss the fact that the Last Supper was held in the context of betrayal*).
- Etc., etc., etc.

In all these examples, which are paradigmatic, we see modeling which leads to rivalry, which leads to violence, which leads to attempted murder or murder! This is especially seen in the first eleven chapters of Genesis where sin and violence fill the earth.

> Genesis 6:11-13 (NASB), "[11] Now the earth was corrupt in the sight of God, and the earth was filled with violence. [12] God looked on the earth, and behold, it was corrupt; for all flesh had corrupted their way upon the earth. [13] Then God said to Noah, 'The end of all flesh has come before Me; for the earth is filled with violence because

of them; and behold, I am about to destroy them with the earth.'"

Consequently, as pastors and leaders, we are models and some of our followers will envy our position, power, authority, etc., and become our rivals. No one really knows why envy, jealousy, and rivalry develops in someone's heart and we don't have to do anything specific to precipitate those feelings. When we say one "No" to something they want or don't give them ourselves, this can precipitate in their minds an illusion and feelings of being mistreated.

This happens more often than we like to admit, because of the closeness we share with our disciples.

By way of example, I had a minister in my church to whom I gave a great deal, i.e. spiritually, emotionally, monetarily, etc. For almost 30 years, we ministered together. When I asked him/her to step down from one ministry—while still holding another ministry—this minister turned on me, talked about me to other members, and eventually left the church in a spirit of offense.

I'm dating myself with this reference, but "There are 10 million stories in the 'Naked City.' You have just heard one of them."

Having become our rivals, some of our followers are willing to do violence to our reputation, authority, etc. to obtain what they covet. If that doesn't get them what they want, they will use murder to get what they want. This murder usually takes place through their trafficking among the members and bad mouthing us as Satan did among the angels, Absalom did among the Israelites, and Judas did with the religious leaders of Israel.

Those who are caught up in mimetic rivalry are blinded by the mechanism and will consider themselves doing the will of God. Again, Girard made a powerful statement that I cannot find the reference for, but nevertheless, he stated, "We are never more blind than when we are doing violence in the name of God!"

Furthermore, our followers become our rivals because they are unwilling to wait or mature to accept something that can only be received as a gift from God, not grasped, clutched, or taken.

Now one of the reasons that this catches us so off guard is because this paradigm has <u>not</u> been recognized. Therefore, we are shocked, even though Peter warns us in

> 1 Peter 4:12-14 (NASB), "[12] Beloved, do not be surprised at the fiery ordeal among you, which comes upon you for your testing, as though some strange thing were happening to you; [13] but to the degree that you share the sufferings of Christ, keep on rejoicing, so that also at the revelation of His glory you may rejoice with exultation. [14] If you are reviled for the name of Christ, you are blessed, because the Spirit of glory and of God rests on you."

We should be expecting betrayal, as it is a human paradigm that is demonstrated all through the Bible and supremely in the life of Jesus!

This leaves us with one question, "How should we respond to betrayal?"

First, our response can be changed by our expectation. Because we have unrealistic expectations of loyalty from our followers, we are usually burned out when betrayal occurs. Unrealistic expectations lead to burnout!

Second, because the same DNA that is in our betrayers is in us, we must be careful not to respond with the same violence and murder. Without realizing it, our dynamic rapport with our disciples may cause us to imitate their violence rather than them imitate our forgiveness and love! Often, without realizing it, even as our betrayers are blinded, we blindly respond in reciprocal violence.

Third, we have the supreme response to betrayal, and it is modeled in the response of Jesus, upon the cross. His response to His betrayers is love and forgiveness. This is the scandal of the cross! His words are, "Father forgive them, because they don't know what they are doing?"

His first response is forgiveness and love! That is the only Christian response to betrayal and the only effective response to violence, because violence only breeds and begets more violence.

In this response, Jesus reveals something about the betrayers, i.e. that they didn't know what they were doing. Well, it looks like they know what they are doing from my point of view! This has always baffled me, but Girard helped me to understand Jesus' statement with this teaching, again "We are never more blind than when we are doing violence in the name of God!"

So, our response to betrayal, in the leitmotif of our Model, Jesus, the Christ, should be love and forgiveness!

Girard and Oughourlian believe that the Bible shows that desire and rivalry can<u>not</u> be separated. Mimetic desire creates rivalry and rivalry exacerbates desire.

They also believe that if you can become aware of this mimetic mechanism, you are on your way to overcoming it!

Rivalry often gives way to violence, but Jesus condemns violence and only reveals one desire: to please the Father.

Our only desire should be to follow Jesus and please the Father.

In conclusion, please consider the following truths that point us towards reducing our blindness and susceptibility to betrayal.

They are taken from Oughourlian's book on marriage, but they are applicable to all relationships.

- We are most vulnerable where we sense a deep need that seemingly can only be filled by the being of another.
- We can only legitimately and healthily be filled by God.
- Therefore, we need to stop trying to fill ourselves with our mates or others.
- We need to stop seeing ourselves as different from and better than our mates or others.
- We need to make sure that God alone is our Model.
- We must accept the reality of mimetic rivalry and seek wisdom.
- We must team up against the devil, rather than allow him to divide us and set us against each other.

- We must learn to love the one that we're with.
- We must renounce a relationship of force for a relationship of love.
- We must seek to reduce rivalry.

This is a brief explanation of betrayal, which I pray will pull the cover off of the mechanism, facilitate an expectation of betrayal, and prepare all people to seek to respond like Jesus.

Prayer

Most gracious heavenly Father, I pray that you will reveal the truths of this book to the readers. I pray for healing for all who have suffered the poison of betrayal. Work grief and forgiveness into their lives.

In addition, open their eyes that they might spiritually discern the mechanism and see betrayal for what it is!

Prepare their hearts that they might not have unrealistic expectations of people in their relationships, but that they might have healthy expectations with respect to betrayal.

I pray that when they are betrayed, they might walk in the footsteps of our Lord and Savior and respond with love and forgiveness.

I believe that You are already at work in the lives of the readers and have providentially led them to this book.

I praise you, in advance, for their deliverance and victory.

In Jesus' name,
Amen!

BIBLIOGRAPHY OF BOOKS I READ ON GIRARD

The Scapegoat	René Girard (translated by Yvonne Freccero)
I See Satan Fall Like Lightening	René Girard
Violence and the Sacred	René Girard
Things Hidden Since the Foundation of the World	René Girard
The Mimetic Brain	Jean-Michel Oughourlian
Deceit, Desire & the Novel: Self and Other in Literary Structure	René Girard
The Genesis of Desire	Jean-Michel Oughourlian
The Theory of René Girard: A Very Simple Introduction	Carly Osborn
Discovering Girard	Michael Kirwan
Job: the Victim of his People	René Girard

CPSIA information can be obtained
at www.ICGtesting.com
Printed in the USA
BVHW071449080719
552849BV00017B/1384/P